INTERESTING FACTS ABOUT
GLACIERS

GEOLOGY FOR BEGINNERS

CHILDREN'S GEOLOGY BOOKS

BABY PROFESSOR
EDUCATION KIDS

Speedy Publishing LLC
40 E. Main St. #1156
Newark, DE 19711
www.speedypublishing.com

In this book, we're going to talk about what glaciers are and how they form. So, let's get right to it!

Above Glacier Grey - Torres Del Paine, Patagonia.

WHAT IS A GLACIER?

A glacier is an enormous layer of ice that covers a landmass. Glaciers cover about 10% of all the land on Earth. Many of these glaciers are at the poles, but there are also some that are positioned at the tops of mountainous ranges. The Himalayan mountain range as well as the Andes both have glaciers.

Glaciers form in areas of the world where the amount of snow that melts to water in the summer is less than the amount of snow that covers the area in the winter. This imbalance builds the amount of ice up gradually year after year. You can think of a glacier as a huge river composed of ice.

Global warming has caused some of these massive flowing ice forms to begin to melt. Greenland's ice cap is made up of enormous glaciers. If the temperature were to warm up to the point that these melted completely, all of land on Earth would be under over 15 feet of water!

Ngozumba Glacier, frozen lakes and Cholatse in spring.

As the layers of ice continue to build up, they begin to compress, which makes them heavier and heavier. Antarctica's glaciers weigh so much that they actually have an impact on the shape of the Earth! Over 70% of all the world's fresh water is frozen in glaciers.

Beautiful view of idyllic summer landscape in the Alps with Gornergrat glacier and highest swiss peaks Nordend and Dufourspitze.

Hubbard Glacier in Alaska.

ICE AGES SHAPED THE EARTH

An ice age happens when ice on the poles starts to increase because the global temperature has lowered. Geologists believe that the Earth has gone through at least five distinct ice ages. They've been able to figure this out by studying the geology of landmasses.

Enormous glaciers shape the surface of the land once they begin to move. There are features all over the world that can only be explained by the movements of glaciers.

Another way that geologists can figure out past ice ages is by studying the chemicals embedded in rocks and the evidence from fossils.

The five major periods that can be categorized as ice ages are:

- **The Huronian Ice Age,** which started 2400 million years ago and lasted 300 million years.

- **The Cryogenian Ice Age,** which started 850 million years ago and lasted over 200 millon years.

Man ice climbing in crevasse.

- **The Andean-Saharan Ice Age,** which started 460 million years ago and lasted over 30 million years.

- **The Karoo Ice Age,** which started 360 million years ago and lasted about 100 million years.

- **The Quarternary Ice Age,** which started about 2.5 million years ago and is still continuing to-day.

Each ice age has two distinct periods of time—a glacial time when the glaciers are in the process of getting larger and an interglacial time period.

Grey Glacier in patagonia.

During the interglacial time period, the glaciers are melting slightly or receding, so the temperatures are a little warmer over all when compared to glacial time periods.

The interglacial time period we're currently in is called the Holocene period. As early as 20,000 years ago a large portion of the country of Canada was covered with ice.

Tidewater Glacier.

Hohe Tauern National Park - Austria.

WHAT CAUSES AN ICE AGE?

There are many factors either singly or jointly that can cause an ice age to occur.

We can't see these things happening, but scientists have data that can show these trends.

THE ORBIT OF THE EARTH

The Earth's orbit changes. At times, we're closer to the Sun and at times we're further away. When we are further away, the temperature drops slightly, which can jumpstart an ice age.

THE ENERGY OF THE SUN

The Sun isn't always consistent in the amount of energy it emits. Low energy cycles can also start an ice age on Earth.

THE AMOUNT OF CARBON DIOXIDE IN THE ATMOSPHERE

Just as high levels of carbon dioxide can contribute to global warming, low levels of CO_2 can cause temperatures to cool, which can lead to an ice age.

El Calafate, Argentina.

THE MOVEMENT AND TEMPERATURE OF OCEAN CURRENTS

Ocean currents, both their movement and temperature, have a huge influence on our planet's climate. These changes can cause ice sheets to start increasing.

The Grey Glacier viewed from a boat.

THE ACTIVITY OF VOLCANOES AROUND THE WORLD

Volcanoes have a direct impact on the amount of carbon dioxide in the atmosphere. If there is very little volcanic activity, it can result in an ice age. On the other hand, too much volcanic activity can result in an excess amount of carbon dioxide, which can result in rising temperatures that end an ice age.

Grey Glacier in chile.

Nigardsbreen glacier, Norway.

HOW DO GLACIERS FORM?

When a huge amount of snow lasts on the ground and doesn't melt for over a year it forms the beginnings of a glacier. This special layer of year-old snow is called a névé. After the snow has existed for over one winter season, it's reached the first stage.

As more snow piles on top of the existing snow over the years, the weight gets heavier and heavier and the snow begins to turn to ice.

Eventually, the compression from the weight is so great that air is even squeezed out of the ice. This is why glaciers have a distinctive blue color. This process of snow layering and becoming ice can take hundreds if not thousands of years.

Perito Moreno Glacier.

HOW DO GLACIERS MOVE?

Once a glacier gets to a certain weight, it starts moving. There are two types of movements that glaciers do, but most movement of glaciers is a mixture of these two types.

SPREADING

This type of movement begins when the glacier can't support its own weight. It starts expanding on all its edges and spreading outward.

Ice, Water, and Rock.

BASAL SLIP

This type of movement occurs when a glacier is positioned on a slope. Mounting pressures cause a thin layer of ice at the bottom part of the glacier to begin melting. Just this thin layer of moving water is enough to get the glacier to begin sliding down the slope.

Sometimes loose soil under a glacier can cause this type of slip to happen as well. The top of a glacier moves more quickly than the bottom of the glacier, due to friction.

Glacial Blue Ice.

When a glacier moves, it moves very, very slowly in a similar way to the way a flowing river moves, only in slow motion. This is because the ice layers are still quite flexible even though they are under enormous pressure. The upper layers of the glacier are the most brittle and tend to crack.

It's very dangerous to walk on the surface of a glacier since fractures can occur. These fractures can form gigantic cracks that can be covered by fresh snow and remain unseen.

Glacier Calving - Natural Phenomenon.

Different glaciers travel at different rates of speed. Some may be fast and travel quite a few feet every day. Others will only travel that much over the course of a year.

A *"retreating glacier"* is one that isn't actually moving backward, but instead is melting more rapidly than gaining ice. When a glacier is moving faster than is typical, it's called a *"surge."*

Glacial Blue Ice.

Calving Glacier.

WHAT ARE THE DIFFERENT TYPES OF GLACIERS?

Geologists have named different types of glaciers.

CALVING

Some glaciers end in bodies of water like oceans or lakes. At times, sheets of ice or icebergs will break off and fall into the water. This process is called "calving." If the water the iceberg breaks into has ocean tides, then the glacier might also be considered a tidewater glacier.

CIRQUE

A glacier that forms on the slopes of a mountain is called a Cirque, Alpine, or Mountain Glacier.

HANGING

Between two mountains sometimes a glacial valley spans. Glaciers that cover the sides of a mountain and hang above the glacier in the valley are called hanging glaciers.

Landscape of the glacier on Monte Rosa, Italy.

ICE CAP

Ice caps cover a landmass with so many layers of ice that even mountains don't poke through.

PIEDMONT

When a glacier overflows into a plain that is located at a mountain range's edge, then it's called a piedmont glacier.

POLAR

Polar glaciers form in regions where the temperature constantly remains below freezing.

Grey Glacier - Torres Del Paine, Patagonia.

TEMPERATE

A glacier that has liquid water is called a temperate glacier. Its ice is at the melting point throughout its entire mass, so the mass it loses is because of melting.

VALLEY

A glacier that is located in the valley of two mountains is called a valley glacier.

Man looks curiously at glacial moulin.

FEATURES OF GLACIERS

ACCUMULATION ZONE

The area where snow falls and collects on the glacier. It's separated from the zone called the ablation zone by an equilibrium line.

ABLATION ZONE

This zone is located below the accumulation area and the firn. This is where the processes of melting and evaporation decrease the amount of ice.

CREVASSES

Deep cracks on a glacier's surfaces are called crevasses. These areas are generally where the glacier is moving more rapidly.

FIRN

The compressed snow that is located between new snow and the ice that forms the glacier is called Firn.

Man leans back to photograph glacier crevasse.

HEAD

The place where the glacier begins is called its Head.

TERMINUS

The glacier's end is called the Terminus or Glacier Foot.

Awesome! Now you know more about the geology of glaciers. You can find more Geology books from Baby Professor by searching the website of your favorite book retailer.

Visit

BABY PROFESSOR
EDUCATION KIDS

www.BabyProfessorBooks.com

to download Free Baby Professor eBooks
and view our catalog of new and exciting
Children's Books

CPSIA information can be obtained
at www.ICGtesting.com
Printed in the USA
BVHW091553020622
638642BV00004B/411

9 781541 938182